# RESISTING
# LEVIATHAN

# RESISTING LEVIATHAN

*The Case Against a European State*

**Philip Vander Elst**

**The Claridge Press**
**London**

First published in Great Britain 1991

by The Claridge Press
6 Linden Gardens
London W2 4ES
and Box 420
Lexington
Georgia 30648


Copyright    ©    Philip Vander Elst    1991

Published with the assistance of the Hampden Trust.

Typeset by
JCL
Frome
and printed by
Short Run Press
Exeter, Devon

ISBN 1-870626-96-6

Vander Elst, Philip: *Resisting Leviathan: The Case Against a European State*


1. Politics

# RESISTING LEVIATHAN

## *The Case Against a European State*

The worst difficulties from which we suffer do not come from without. They come from within. They ... come from the mood of unwarrantable self-abasement into which we have been cast by a powerful section of our own intellectuals .... Nothing can save England if she will not save herself. If we lose faith in ourselves, in our capacity to guide and to govern, if we lose our will to live, then indeed our story is told.

SIR WINSTON CHURCHILL 1933[1]

The dream of Internationalism, the reaching out of Europeans towards each other, and of Europe towards the world, has awakened to an alarming reality: the creation of a whole new layer of government superimposed upon the layers of government we already have. Supranationality is, quite predictably, producing exactly the opposite results from that at which internationality aims. Power being delightful, and profitable, governments and bureaucracies tend to expand. To extend the powers of Brussels would be to put ourselves under a power whose future course we could not predict, and it would not even have the effect of diminishing the powers already exercised over us by national governments.

PROFESSOR KENNETH MINOGUE[2]

## Introduction

Half a century ago, when Britain was fighting for her life and the freedom of Europe, no important body of opinion would have questioned the value of patriotism or the importance of preserving and cherishing our nationhood as a focus of resistance to Nazi totalitarianism. Pride in our heritage, our sense of connection with the past and with the achievements of our forebears, were not only second nature to millions of people in the Britain of 1940, but were widely shared throughout the English-speaking world and helped to mobilise opinion against Hitler. Men and women in the United States and the British Dominions drew strength and inspiration in these years of crisis from their common historical and cultural roots, and these were celebrated in literature and song, on the screen and printed page, from one end of the world to the other. Penguin Books, to cite a typical example, published two anthologies during this period — *Portrait of England* and *Forever Freedom* — which are a treasure trove of prose and verse celebrating our Island story. They sing the praises of our countryside and institutions, our traditions and people, in the words of Shakespeare and Milton, Emerson and Whittier, Burke and Jefferson, and countless others. Today, however, such sentiments strike a jarring note and are generally ridiculed as outdated and narrow-minded. The nation state, we are told, has outlived its usefulness, and moral idealism dictates that all enlightened people should favour its absorption into a supra-national European bloc in the name of what is misleadingly called 'Europeanism'. Others go even further and look forward to the eventual creation of a world state which will supposedly remove violence and war from the lives of nations. Whilst these two groups only partially overlap, they are united in the belief that their vision reflects the tide of history, and that it is useless to swim against it.

This pamphlet, by contrast, accepts none of these arguments. If the tide of history is flowing in the wrong direction, it is the duty of any sensible person to try and arrest its course rather than to swim with it in the spirit of Vichy and Quisling. This 'blast' is therefore aimed at the 'ships' seeking to catch this treacherous tide, with the intention of holing them below the water line. In particular, it hopes to persuade their confused passengers of the truth of the following propositions: first, the trend towards supra-nationalism is not an expression of true *internationalism*, of that generous sympathy and spirit of co-operation which can only be rooted in the widening rather than the destruction of patriotism. Secondly, the belief that nationalism is the principal cause of conflict and war is both historically inaccurate and politically naive. And third, the glory of Europe and the secret of her creativity and dynamism as a civilisation has lain in decentralisation and diversity rather than in size and empire. Finally, and perhaps most important, the attempt to create a European State which would incorporate Britain, is not only harmful to our interests and incompatible with all that is best in our heritage and traditions; it would also be bad for democracy and would, in the long run, endanger freedom. Most ironically of all, it would almost certainly intensify rather than reduce national tensions within Europe, and it would probably damage world trade and harm the interests of Third World countries — an effect the European Community is already having in its pre-federalist form through its Common Agricultural Policy.

# The Implications of European Federalism

## The Issue of Sovereignty

Despite the importance attached to the subject of 'Europe' by the 'great and the good', the British electorate's relative lack of interest in it is regularly demonstrated in opinion polls, in which domestic issues like 'inflation', or the 'National Health Service', predominate. The low British turn-out in European Parliamentary elections is a similarly eloquent symbol of popular apathy towards this enterprise, yet the future of Europe and of Britain's place in it is the most important single question in British politics. As such, it should be brought into the centre of public discussion since it affects, directly or indirectly, nearly every other social and political issue. The reason? One word: *sovereignty*.

Here we run into the first smokescreen obscuring the contours of what ought to be an impassioned national debate, namely, the unwillingness of so-called 'pro-Europeans' to call a spade a spade and admit that the goal of economic and political union is incompatible with the retention of Britain's sovereignty and independence as a nation. Their insistent assertion that European union represents a 'sharing' or 'pooling' of national sovereignty, rather than its abandonment, is not only nonsense from a logical standpoint, but is damaging to our democracy since it prevents the British people from reaching a clear understanding of both the stakes and the genuine advantages and disadvantages involved in supra-national empire-building at the European level. This in turn helps to explain the ignorance and apathy surrounding this topic in Britain, unlike the situation on the Continent where politicians are more candid and clear-headed about the political and constitutional implications of European union. For these reasons, we must spell out the consequences for sovereignty inherent in European Federalism and examine the degree to which our national independence is now in jeopardy within the European Community. This is particularly necessary since the Community's architects have never hidden their supra-national objectives, though these have either been misunderstood or concealed from the British electorate by our own 'pro-Europeans'.

The *Concise Oxford Dictionary* defines the word 'unite' in the following terms: "Join together, make or become one, combine, consolidate, *amalgamate*." (author's italics). Consequently, if words retain their normal meaning, European economic and political union necessarily implies a transfer of sovereignty, and of the right to self-government, from the constituent nations of the European Community to some newly created European federal authority. To put it even more bluntly, just as a family loses its independence if its household budget is controlled by outsiders, so a nation loses its freedom of action if decisions about taxation, public expenditure, and monetary policy are transferred to supra-national institutions — a process which is of course reinforced when it embraces defence and foreign policy. It is therefore absurd to talk about 'pooling' or 'sharing' sovereignty, since the acquisition of a right to interfere in the affairs of our European neighbours does not alter the fact that we lose a portion of our independence whenever we submit ourselves to a process of collective decision-making in which we may find ourselves in a minority. *And here we come to the crux of the matter.* The cost of losing sovereignty only becomes apparent when we come into conflict with the majority of our partners and are forced to submit to their views. Consequently, the real issue before us when we contemplate the prospect of European Federalism is not 'Are we going to lose sovereignty?', but: 'Will the surrender of our sovereignty be justified by the benefits obtained from merging our political identity with our eleven European neighbours?' This is a particularly important question for British electors since loss of sovereignty entails the dilution of our votes in a pool of twelve electorates determining the make-up of the European Parliament.

So, are we prepared for that? Is this what we really want or is there a better alternative, more in keeping with our history and with all that is best in European civilisation?

The need to make up our minds about this challenge becomes ever more pressing given the European Community's increasingly explicit advance towards the goal of establishing a 'United States of Europe'.

## The Advance Towards European Federalism

Whatever our own politicians may say and however much they may try to fudge the issue, it is now abundantly clear that a strong federalist current is carrying the European Community towards a destination which has never been approved or even discerned by a majority of our fellow-citizens. Almost daily, speeches are made, conferences held, or proposals put forward which reflect this trend. To give only a few recent examples: the weekly newspaper, *The European*, carried a front page story in its edition of 16-18 November 1990, headed, "Summit's radical plan for a federal Europe — Kohl calls for surrender of sovereignty". The story that followed, by Denise Claveloux, reporting from Brussels, stated: "A powerful group of European leaders, led by Germany's Chancellor Kohl and five prime ministers, were due to approve plans this week-end for a united states of Europe which would include a substantial transfer of sovereignty from national governments and the creation of a common currency by 1997. The plan, which calls for full economic, monetary and political union, goes far beyond the proposals backed by the 11 EC leaders at the Rome Summit last month. It also backs the creation of an EC security and defence policy, and would remove member states' existing right of veto, so that all decisions in the Council of Ministers would be by qualified majority vote..."

In a similar vein, a report from Brussels published in *The Times* on 12th December 1990, revealed that "Protesters will march in Rome on Friday calling for a United States of Europe, the

European Movement said yesterday. They believe the time has come for a European union on a federal base. The movement is holding a convention for European democracy to coincide with the summit." Another report in *The Times*, of 13th December, was headed: "The Road to a united states of Europe", and declared: "Most countries, apart from Britain, now see a need to extend or redefine the jurisdiction of the community. They want drugs, immigration and the control of frontiers, currently covered by informal co-operation among the Twelve, brought into the ambit of a new treaty. They want the Commission to have new powers over social affairs, the environment, education, research and technology, tax, health, culture, tourism, energy, telecommunications and transport networks. They also think that more decisions should be taken by qualified majority vote." To make matters even plainer, an additional article by Michael Binyon, further down the same page, stated: "Economic and monetary union is the most far-reaching change proposed for the European Community since its inception in 1957. It would, the former chancellor Nigel Lawson said last year, inevitably lead to the United States of Europe."

Even before these events and the decisions and declarations of the subsequent European summit in Rome, the federalist ideals behind the establishment of the European Community have been obvious from the beginning. The 1957 Treaty of Rome, for instance, aimed at "the approximation of the laws of the Member States" (Article 3) and expressed the desire to "lay the foundation of an ever closer union among the peoples of Europe." (Recitals). Fourteen years later, in June 1971, these objectives were emphatically reiterated by West Germany's Foreign Minister, Walter Scheel, when he declared: *"the aim remains a European Government ... the argument over a United States of Europe or a Federal Europe is one of words. A European Government will take decisions on common policies and will be subject to a European Parliamentary control."* More recently, on 14th February 1984, the European Parliament adopted, by 231 votes to 31, with 43 abstentions, a Draft Treaty of European Union, proposing — among other things — that "the law of the Union" should be "directly applicable in the Member States" and "should take precedence over national law" (Article 42), and that "the Union should have the power to tax and raise loans" (Article 71), conduct a foreign policy, and should be represented by the Commission and its embassies *vis-a-vis* non-EC states. (Articles 63, 64, 65 and 69) To cap it all, the European Parliament declared that this Draft Treaty should become effective once it had been ratified by two-thirds of the EC's Member States, regardless of the attitudes of the remaining one-third (Article 82).

Against this background, it is totally disingenuous for any British politician to pretend that Britain's independence and sovereignty are not seriously threatened by the current process of European integration, however much that process may be slowed down or modified for a transitional period to accommodate British susceptibilities and the current Conservative Government's need to maintain party unity on this controversial question. As even Michael Heseltine has had to admit, despite his tendency to minimise the conflict between British sovereignty and European integration, "There is no escaping the fact that a fledgling federalism is emerging, however the dictionary definition of this emotive word may be stretched to pretend otherwise. Many may not like it but it cannot be wished away." (*The Challenge of Europe: Can Britain Win?*, M. Heseltine, London, 1989.)

Unfortunately, the opportunity of having an honest debate about federalism, and about the whole direction in which the European Community is evolving, has been denied to the British people for twenty years by the failure of most of our 'pro-European' politicians and pundits to come clean about the potential implications of British membership of the EEC (as it used to be called). Conservative governments and ministers have been particularly glib in dismissing the fears of anti-federalists over the past two decades.

## Fudging The Issue of European Federalism

The Heath Government's 1971 White Paper recommending

Britain's entry into the EEC, for instance, stated: "the Community is no federation" (Cmnd 4715, p.8) and "there is no question of eroding any national sovereignty" (Ibid). In an earlier speech made by Mr Heath in the House of Commons on 25 February 1970, he declared: "There will not be a blueprint for a federal Europe.... What is more, those members of the Community who want a federal system, but who know the views of Her Majesty's Government and the Opposition Parties here, are prepared to forego their federal desires so that Britain should be a member ... I believe this to be of great importance." (*Hansard*, Fifth Series, Vol. 796, col. 1221.)

It is also interesting, in view of his anger against Mrs Thatcher for resisting economic and monetary union — and his consequent role in her downfall — that Sir Geoffrey Howe also denied the federalist danger when replying to debates as Solicitor-General during the passage through the House of Commons of the 1972 European Communities Bill. Asking the rhetorical question: "What is the position concerning the ultimate supremacy of Parliament?" (*Hansard*, Fifth Series, Vol. 840, col. 627), he answered: "the position is that the ultimate supremacy of Parliament will not be affected." (*Ibid.*) Fourteen years later, during the debate in Parliament over the 1986 Single European Act, Sir Geoffrey, as Foreign Secretary, unequivocally stated: "we are not talking about the declaration or proclamation of a United States of Europe." (*Hansard*, Sixth Series, Vol. 96, col. 325.)

The time for neglect and evasion in confronting the challenge of European federalism has come to an end. If we wish to determine our own future as a nation and preserve our independence and freedom of action in the days to come, we must consciously resist incorporation into a United States of Europe. If, furthermore, we wish to safeguard the liberty, diversity and creativity which have been the life-blood of European civilisation as a whole — and not just of our own country — we must understand why a federalist destiny would be a betrayal rather than the fulfilment of the European ideal.

# In Defence of Patriotism and Nationhood

The sympathy of England with liberty, and with the freedom and independence of communities and nationalities, is of ancient origin, and has become the traditional direction of our foreign policy.... It was mainly English effort which rescued Germany and the Netherlands from the despotism of King Philip of Spain, and after him from that of Louis XIV of France.  It was English effort which preserved the liberties of Europe from the desolating tyranny of Napoleon.  In our own times our own nation has done much, either by direct intervention or by energetic moral support, to establish upon firm foundations the freedom of Italy and of Greece.

LORD RANDOLPH CHURCHILL 1886[3]

Lord, while for all mankind we pray,
    Of every clime and coast,
O hear us for our native land,
    The land we love the most ...

J.R. WREFORD 1800-1881[4]

As these expressions of nineteenth century English patriotism suggest, nothing is sillier or more superficial than the endlessly repeated argument that nationalism is the principal cause of discord between peoples, and that the best guarantee of peace in Europe would be the creation of a layer of supra-national government controlling formerly independent nations and supposedly embodying a new spirit of unity and goodwill.  Logic and history combine to refute this simplistic view.

In the first place, it ought to be self-evident that a man's love for his country does not automatically imply that he hates or despises someone else's, any more than his love for his family necessarily

implies hostility towards his neighbour. Human sympathy and
feelings of solidarity are naturally strongest when they reflect a
sense of common interest and identity rooted in shared values and a
common heritage, but that does not mean that they remain confined
within those limits. Thus we first develop our sense of connection
with others within those "little platoons" about which Burke waxed
so eloquent — within our families, regions and localities. But then,
by a natural process of experience and discovery, we perceive our
links with a wider community and learn to identify with the country
and nation whose language and culture shape our minds and lives.
If, in addition, we have grown up in a free democracy, we also learn
to identify with other societies which share our commitment to
liberty and the rule of law — especially if, like Canada or the United
States, they are linked to us historically as former colonies. Human
sympathy, in other words, grows naturally out of a widening circle
of association, and the very fact that we love our country and are
proud of its best achievements and traditions, helps us to appreciate
the patriotic sensibilities and feelings of others and can bring out the
best in us rather than the worst. As that great-hearted Conservative
statesman, Arthur Balfour, put it earlier this century, in his lecture
on 'Nationality and Home Rule':

> The sentiment of nationality is one of a group of such sentiments for
> which there is unfortunately no common name. Loyalties to a country,
> a Party, a constitution, a national sovereign, a tribal chief, a church, a
> pact, a creed, are characteristic specimens of the class. They may be
> ill-directed; they often are. Nevertheless it is such loyalties that make
> human society possible; they do more, they make it noble. To them we
> owe it that a man will sacrifice ease, profit, life itself, for something
> which wholly transcends his merely personal interests. Therefore,
> whether mistaken or not, there is in them always a touch of greatness.
> But it has to be observed that the kind of loyalty we call patriotism,
> though it expresses a simple feeling, need have no exclusive application.
> It may embrace a great deal more than a man's country or a man's race.
> It may embrace a great deal less. And these various patriotisms need
> not be, and should not be, mutually exclusive.

It is not a coincidence then, that this Scottish and British patriot should have felt a generous sympathy for the national aspirations of the Jews after centuries of suffering and exile. It is not strange that he should have lent his name to that famous declaration of 1917 promising British support for the re-establishment of a Jewish homeland in Palestine. Nor is it surprising, as the words of Lord Randolph Churchill reveal, that patriotic liberal England in the nineteenth century openly defended and supported the emerging liberal and national movements in Italy, Greece and Belgium, as an earlier England had fought side by side with the Dutch against the imperial armies of King Philip in the sixteenth century. It was patriotic empathy, a belief in liberty, and a sense of reverence and gratitude for her matchless heritage, which moved Byron to participate in Greece's struggle for independence from the tyranny of the Ottoman empire. That was the spirit which inspired such famous lines as these, from his poem, 'The Isles of Greece':

The mountains look on Marathon —
    And Marathon looks on the sea;
And musing there an hour alone,
    I dreamed that Greece might still be free;
For standing on the Persian's grave,
    I could not deem myself a slave.

Not only, then, is it absurd on a theoretical level to regard patriotism and loyalty to the nation state as the chief cause of hatred and conflict between countries, but it is also unhistorical. With the exception of tribal conflicts within primitive communities and continents, more wars have been caused by religious and ideological passions and by the dynastic ambitions of powerful princes than by the forces of popular nationalism. The wars of the Middle Ages, for instance, were usually either family quarrels between contending monarchs related to each other by blood or marriage, or struggles for power between these monarchs and their rebellious barons, or between the Pope, representing the Church, and the Holy Roman Emperor or some other secular ruler. Later on, the earthquake of the

Reformation ushered in more than a century of bloody religious strife between Protestants and Catholics, whilst Central Europe and the Balkans were the scene of a recurring conflict between Islam and Christianity, echoing in its fierce intensity the costly battles in Palestine between Christian and Saracen during the early Crusades.

It is therefore not only untrue to portray nationalism as the inevitable or principal progenitor of war; it is also unfair, given the fact that some wars have been caused by attempts to *suppress* rather than advance popular nationalism. As one modern historian and critic of European Federalism (Dr Alan Sked) has pointed out:

> ... nationalism has many advantages: it reconciles classes; smooths over regional differences; and gives ordinary people a sense of community, pride and history. European nationalists are themselves seeking precisely those benefits from *THE* European Ideal'. It is therefore ironic that they should blame nation-state nationalists exclusively for war. For a strict account of modern European history would show that it was largely the refusal of supra-national, dynastic states — the Ottoman, Habsburg and Napoleonic empires — to allow for national self-determination which brought about wars. Likewise, in the twentieth century, it was the Kaiser's bid for world power ... and Hitler's racial mumbo-jumbo which led to world conflict. In short, it has been the apparent redundancy of the nation-state and the yearning for continental power-bases which in previous centuries has more than once led to the negation of 'European Civilisation'.[5]

This leads us to the real heart of the matter, which is that the chief cause of hatred and war is not nationalism or national diversity but fallen human nature — or the radical imperfection of the human condition, if one wants to put it in more secular terms. "Out of the heart come evil thoughts", says Christ in the New Testament (Matthew 15: 19); and when flawed human nature is tempted and corrupted by excessive power, the results are as disastrous for international relations as they are inimical to peace and liberty internally. Hence, as Dr Sked's comment reveals, it is the appetite for power of tyrannical rulers or castes which is the common factor in many conflicts, and that appetite may be aroused or buttressed by an intolerant and aggressive ideology which has nothing to do with patriotism or nationalism in the ordinary sense. The millions who died, for instance, in the great European and world conflagrations of the late eighteenth and early nineteenth centuries, and in those of our own terrible era, were the victims of Jacobinism, Bonapartism, National Socialism and Communism — of movements and ideologies which transcended normal national loyalties and appealed instead, or as much, to race, class, hero-worship, or utopianism. Consequently, the great lesson they teach us is the opposite of the one drawn by European Federalists and contemporary advocates of supra-nationalism. Far from being the key to opening the Pandora Box of war, loyalty to the nation state is one of the pillars of a free and peaceful international order, since it represents a focus of sentiment which is decentralised and which is therefore an obstacle to the construction of totalitarian power blocs and the spread of totalitarian ideologies. Furthermore, by inculcating a love of country in the hearts of men and women, nationalism helps to motivate people to defend their inherited rights and freedoms, and so mobilises powerful emotional forces against actual and potential oppression. What else saved Britain in 1940 and eventually defeated Hitler?

Whilst it may be understandable that the 'European' advocates of federalism should fail to see the link between patriotism and freedom, it is nonetheless ironic that they should have forgotten the salutary words of one of the greatest European political philosophers. Two hundred years ago, Montesquieu wrote, in his famous treatise, *De l'Ésprit Des Lois:*

> In Asia they have always had great empires: in Europe these could never subsist. Asia has larger plains; it is cut into much more extensive divisions by mountains and seas ... in Europe, the natural division forms many nations of a moderate extent, in which the ruling by laws is not incompatible with the maintenance of the state.... It is this which has formed a genius for liberty, that renders every part extremely difficult to be subdued and subjected by a foreign power.

Since we can be sure that Montesquieu's conclusion would strike a responsive chord in those Eastern European countries freeing themselves from the 'internationalist' yoke of Soviet Communism, it is even more ironic to hear European Federalists announcing the end of the nation state at precisely the time when our fellow Europeans in the East are rediscovering and repossessing their national independence and heritage. It is also a monument to inconsistency, since the same 'progressive' and 'liberal' circles typically support 'African nationalism' and other 'national liberation' movements in the Third World, despite the fact that these brands of 'nationalism', or tribalism, are the most tyrannical, destructive and chauvinistic of the modern world — unredeemed as they are by Western traditions of civility, tolerance and liberty.

The truth is that ever since the First World War, a majority of our intellectuals has ceaselessly denigrated our national heritage and traditions, and devoted enormous energy and resources to the subversion and destruction of our sense of national identity. Overreacting to the narrowness, arrogance, and philistinism which tainted some of the expressions of patriotism in this country at the turn of the century, our 'chattering classes' have drawn the wrong lessons from two world wars and have taught an increasing number of people to regard even legitimate feelings of national pride as a form of 'racism', as being somehow incompatible with respect for other nationalities. Not surprisingly, this has helped to sap our national morale and persuade many in our society to lend an ear to the voices of defeatism, which tell us that we cannot survive or prosper in the modern world unless we surrender our independence in return for membership of a larger supra-national state. On this farrago of nonsense we must now turn our guns if we are to remove the blinkers of national self-doubt currently preventing people from seeing the dangers of European Federalism.

## Britain's Place In The World:  Countering Defeatism

In 1859, another great Conservative statesman encapsulated the truth about Britain's place in the world in a speech at Aylesbury. In it he declared:

> Remember always that England, though she is bound to Europe by tradition, by affection, by great similarity of habits, and all those ties which time alone can create and consecrate, is not a mere power of the Old World. Her geographical position, her laws, her language and religion connect her as much with the New World as with the Old. Still if ever Europe by her shortsightedness falls into an inferior or exhausted state, for England there will remain an illustrious future. We are bound to the communities of the New World, and those great States which our own planting and colonizing energies have created, by ties and interests which will sustain our power, and enable us to play as great a part in the times yet to come, as we do in these days, and as we have done in the past.[6]

Looking back at these words of Disraeli's, one is astonished, at one level, by their prescience. Here we have, nearly a century before the events in question, an exact description of the way in which Britain's ties with the United States and with the Old Dominions of Australia, New Zealand and Canada, played a crucial role not only in our deliverance from invasion and blockade in 1940-41, but also in the liberation of Europe and Asia from the tyranny of the Axis Powers. At another level, however, there is no reason for surprise. Disraeli only voiced what common sense reveals about Britain's historic ties and geo-strategic position, namely that as a maritime Mid-Atlantic trading power, with close ties to the great English-speaking democracies of the Atlantic and Pacific basins, she has wider interests and connections than her continental neighbours, and cannot place herself in a European straightjacket without damage to her political and economic future.

Britain's traditional need for free trade and her perennial interest in preventing the domination of the European landmass by a single hostile or unfriendly power, be it a country or a regional bloc, is as great today as it has ever been, and what is more, serves the needs and interests of other countries. To start with, every nation benefits from unhampered world trade, especially the poorer and weaker ones desperate for foreign investment and for overseas markets for their agricultural products. Everyone would therefore be threatened, politically as well as commercially, by the emergence of an international order dominated by strong supra-national regional states. To allow such a development would be a recipe for bullying and protectionism in a world in which the temptation to placate powerful lobbies and throw one's weight around at the expense of others is as widespread as it is. That is why Britain's greatest leaders have shared a common perception of where her true interests lie. That is why Sir Winston Churchill, for example, held the same view of Britain's destiny as Disraeli, and did *not* support her membership of a United Europe — despite the attempt of Tories like Sir Geoffrey Howe to suggest otherwise. As Churchill put it at the beginning of the 1950s:

> We are with Europe, but not of it. We are linked, but not combined. We are interested and associated,but not absorbed. And should European statesmen address us in the words which were used of old — 'Shall I speak for thee to the King or the Captain of the Host?' — we should reply with the Shunamite woman: 'Nay, sir, for we dwell among our own people.'[7]

Unfortunately, the obvious facts about Britain's place in the world, and her permanent interests, have been obscured by two decades of defeatist propaganda about her supposed inability to 'stand alone' outside 'Europe'. Instead of exposing the absurdity of the notion that a Britain which trades freely with nearly every country in the world, belongs to NATO, the OECD and other groupings, risks 'isolation' unless she joins a supra-national 'European Club', our political establishment has, with few exceptions, swallowed the poisoned bait hook, line and sinker, and browbeaten the country into believing that acceptance of such handicaps as the protectionist idiocies of the Common Agricultural Policy, is part of the price of national survival behind the walls of our 'European' shelter. In addition, our leaders have constantly sought to reconcile us to the process of ever deeper European integration, by arguing that it is 'inevitable' and that if we don't go along with it, Britain will be relegated to 'the Second Division' — a theme constantly reiterated by men like Michael Heseltine.

But do we have to be browbeaten in this fashion? The answer is that of course we don't. No-one who reflects upon the fear inspired in Europe and the United States by Japanese competition, or the barriers erected by many countries against imports from Hong Kong, can continue to believe that size is the secret of a country's economic success, or that no country can prosper unless it belongs to some large and powerful supra-national trading bloc. As Tim Congdon, one of our most astute economists and experts on international trade, has written:

> Despite all the rhetoric on the virtues of bigness, there is no connection in the real world between the size of countries and their standards of living. On the contrary, ample evidence could be cited to suggest that small countries are more economically successful than large countries. The highest incomes per head in Europe today are in Switzerland, while for many years the Scandinavian countries have had far better living standards than the European average. In Asia, tiny Singapore and Hong Kong have incomes per head which are a multiple of those in giant China and India.[8]

The real truth is that the secret of 'the wealth of nations' lies in the encouragement of free enterprise and free trade, as Adam Smith taught us long ago and as the failure of Communism has reminded us recently. It does not lie in economic elephantiasis and supra-national empire-building. As Mr Congdon goes on to explain:

> The common feature of countries like Switzerland, Sweden, Singapore and Hong Kong is that they participate actively in international trade.... They all have relatively low levels of tariff protection and avoid other forms of import restriction. Indeed, Singapore and Hong Kong have virtual free trade. As a result, their industries all look outwards to the rest of the world, not inwards to local customers, when they want to sell their products. The distinction between the 'internal' and 'external' market is barely meaningful. Their 'internal market' is not defined by national boundaries or by membership of a regional trading bloc, but

is effectively the world as a whole.[9]

Given the need, then, for maximum British participation in the international economy, it is not in our interests to sacrifice free trade with the rest of the world in order to keep in step with the protectionist policy of the European Community. Rather, a country like ours, which has traditionally bred the independent-minded merchants, craftsmen, poets and adventurers so crucial to the enterprise of an island straddling the sea lanes to four continents, should turn its back on 'little Europeanism' and set its face instead towards the 'open seas' — towards the many lands and climes where British effort and enterprise can best create wealth and earn the legitimate rewards of thrift and ingenuity.

## The Flawed Idealism Behind European Union

Much, perhaps most, of the momentum behind the movement towards European Union, is idealistic rather than materialistic — despite the unsavoury spectacle of a Common Agricultural Policy which sacrifices the interests of poor Third World producers to the political self-interest of vote-buying European politicians. Expediency aside, there is great emotional steam behind the idea of European integration and European Federalism. This is not only generated by the belief that it would put an end to the possibility of another European war, but also derives its intensity from the conviction that a United Europe would somehow embody all that is most precious about European civilisation. But is this really true? Would the establishment of a European state encourage greater harmony between its constituent parts than exists under present arrangements? Would a Federal Union allow sufficient room for that diversity and freedom which Montesquieu considered the essence of Europe? Finally, would a European state respect the rights of national minorities, or would it become too centralised for its own good?

The failure of most British politicians to acknowledge the federalist impulse driving European integration, has resulted in the neglect of these vital questions, but we cannot evade them if we wish to avoid travelling on a train which is moving with increasing speed towards a destination which we have never chosen. If, however, the inner decision to confront them is taken, it soon becomes apparent that the answers contradict the simplistic assumptions of 'European' idealists.

The conviction that the existence of the European Community has maintained the peace in Europe since 1957, is extremely naive. Peace was already an established fact when the EC's founder members signed the Treaty of Rome, and the reason for that lay in the destruction in 1945 of the totalitarian ideology which had seized Germany during the 1930s and caused her to turn on her neighbours at the end of that decade. Furthermore, the guarantee of this post-war peace was, and still is, the deterrent power of the North Atlantic Alliance, buttressed by the presence of American troops in Europe. In addition, the establishment of the Common Market, as the EC used to be called, *reflected* rather than caused the new post-war spirit of Franco-German understanding that was being brought into being by the statesmanship of Adenauer and De Gaulle. As for the friendliness and co-operation which currently exists between the peoples of the Western half of our continent, that has more to do with the personal contacts established through trade, sport, travel and communications, than with the formal institutions erected in Brussels and Strasbourg. Today, even more than in the past, it is the natural processes of capitalism which bind free and democratic nations together. It is no doubt also true that these processes have been greatly reinforced by German guilt about the past and the traumatic lessons learnt in destruction and defeat. To talk therefore of the need for European Union in the cause of peace, effectively amounts to an irrational and unnecessary attempt to prevent the outbreak of the Second World War. It represents a ridiculous attempt not only to shut the stable door when the horse has bolted, but to do so when there is no longer a horse which needs stabling.

The pacifist argument for European Federalism not only lacks credibility and derives its appeal chiefly from unreasoning emotion; it paradoxically enhances the prospect of future strife, by diverting attention from the real ingredients of political and cultural conflict between nations.

Mention was made earlier of the fact that many of the wars which took place in nineteenth century Europe were caused by attempts to suppress rather than encourage nationalism. This highlights the truth that attempts to destroy national heterogeneity inevitably lead to conflict, since the strong attachment people feel for their language, customs, and way of life, provokes resistance against attacks upon the institutions which give them their identity. Consequently, large communities can only hold together if the differences between their citizens are outweighed by what they have in common in the form of shared values and cultural roots, and a common language. For the same reason, large international group-ings can only operate harmoniously if their member nations are allowed sufficient autonomy to preserve both their separate identity and their capacity for self-determination. In a Federal Europe, however, the differences between its constituent states would be far too great to make federalism a workable recipe for supra-national harmony.

Whilst it is true that we are all European nations with a common Christian heritage and democratic institutions, that pre-cious bond is an insufficient basis on which to build a harmonious and workable federal system. To believe otherwise, is to ignore the difficulties inherent in the creation of a supra-national community embracing at least ten different languages and cultures, as well as divergent political traditions. Some of our European partners, for instance, have, in the recent past, known long periods of internal violence, dictatorship and instability, whilst others have only been properly constituted nation states for a fraction of the time that we have. Almost no European country, apart from Britain, has enjoyed three centuries of parliamentary government under a constitutional monarchy. In the equivalent period, France alone has experienced royalist absolutism, revolutionary Jacobinism, two Empires and five republics.

All this is not to indulge in cheap xenophobic sneers. On the other side of the coin, parliamentary democracy has been flourishing in Germany to an extent that would once have been regarded as incredible, and the Dutch, like the British, have known a long period of constitutional and parliamentary government. The point is simply that the nucleus of a common liberal tradition is not sufficiently strong and well established to support a liberal supranational state. Consequently, the effort to construct a United States of Europe cannot be compared with the establishment of the United States of America, or the Canadian federation, where linguistic and cultural homogeneity were far more pronounced from the outset, and where political development was almost exclusively shaped by English ideals of liberty and Anglo-Saxon Common Law. Furthermore, even these cases underline the problems inherent in the creation of large federal states, since federal union did not prevent a terribly costly American Civil War in the 1860s, and the Canadian federation is in constant danger of collapse over the thorny question of French-speaking Quebec.

## The Potential Threat To Democracy And Freedom

The problem of heterogeneity within a Federal Europe is particularly serious because it affects the workings of democracy, since in any democratic system, the willingness of minorities to abide by majority rule is influenced by the degree to which all citizens feels a sense of belonging to the same community. If, however, dissident minorities have to accept unpalatable decisions imposed by a majority composed of other nationalities, the pill becomes much harder to swallow and the resulting tensions much greater —as the example of Yugoslavia graphically demonstrates. Consequently, it is more than probable that a Federal Europe embracing Britain and all the existing states within the European Community, would impose greater strains on the loyalties of its member countries than are currently experienced within the Community in its pre-federalist form. This in turn could lead, in the future, either to bitter conflict followed by the secession of one or more of the member states, or to the creation of a stronger and more authoritarian federal government determined to stamp out the glowing embers of national separatism.

The difficulties for democracy posed by European Federalism do not, unfortunately, end here. European Union would also have the disadvantage of reducing our capacity as voters and citizens to influence the institutions which govern our lives. However liberal the constitution of a federal state may be, the creation of a geographically more extensive political community inevitably means that the centre of power and decision-making becomes more remote from the individual citizen — both geographically and institutionally. It becomes that much harder to bring pressure to bear on bureaucrats and politicians. Not only is the competition for attention and influence more intense, but the ability to punish governments by securing their defeat at the polls is reduced because the electoral pool is much larger. Hence, if the present European Community becomes a federal state, it will mean that every vote cast by a British elector in a general election will be diluted by a factor of twelve. The decision of the British electorate as a whole will be similarly swamped by those of the other eleven, and the numerical odds will only lengthen against us if more countries join the federal union. Add to that the extra difficulty for pressure groups of having to urge their case within a community embracing different languages and cultural outlooks, and the democratic argument against incorporation into a European superstate becomes overwhelming.

Examination of the problems for democracy inherent in the movement towards European Federalism, emphasises the blind spot of those idealists who try to persuade us of the benefits of European Union by describing the advantages that would flow from the adoption of beneficial policies on a larger European scale. Whilst it is obvious that we might all favour a Europe made in our own image, the fly in the ointment is that we would not have the power to transform our vision into reality. Others might, almost certainly would, have other ideas, and the Europe that would eventually emerge might bear little resemblance to the Europe of our dreams. Already today, within the existing European Community — as the GATT negotiations have demonstrated — Britain's traditional interest in free trade with the United States, and with other non-European countries, has been compromised by her need to keep in step with the commercial policy of the EC as a whole. Differences have similarly emerged between Britain and her European neighbours over the proper handling of the recent Gulf Crisis, with her partners taking a noticeably softer line towards Iraqi aggression. Does this not suggest that a common European foreign policy might weaken rather than strengthen the external position of the Western democracies?

These reflections bring us, finally, to the most important strand of the argument against Euro-federalism, which is that the creation of a European state would ultimately endanger freedom.

While no one doubts the good faith or commitment to democracy of the present supporters of European Union, history suggests that, human nature being what it is, an enlargement of the political stage is likely to increase the opportunities and temptations to abuse power. Even if the tyrannical propensities of a future European government were no greater than those of a national one, the loss of freedom would be more widespread and serious in the event that democracy collapsed. And while that prospect may seem far-fetched in 1991, it should not be dismissed in a continent which has experienced the ravages of Marxism and Fascism in the historically recent past, and in which — as has already been mentioned — few countries possess Britain's long tradition of peaceful evolutionary change and liberal constitutional government.

The truth is that liberty is a rare and fragile plant which can only grow in certain cultural soils and which quickly withers if the conditions necessary for its preservation are neglected or changed. Even in historically successful liberal communities, like the United States — with its Bill of Rights and written constitution — central government has had a built-in tendency to increase its jurisdiction and authority as it has sought or obtained new functions to cope with new problems. There are always ambitious politicians seeking to buy votes with the taxpayer's money, and government bureaucrats and employees with a vested interest in extending the powers of the State. It is consequently never wise to ignore the dangers of centralising power, which is why the current trend towards supra-nationalism is so disquieting.

## An Alternative Vision Of European Co-operation

Do these reflections imply rejection of the need for closer international co-operation in various fields? Of course they don't. But they teach us to distinguish between supra-nationalism and *internationalism*. And in a century which has demonstrated that more people have been killed in internal repression within totalitarian socialist states than have died in two world wars,[10] that is a lesson we ignore at our peril. It is one thing to seek closer and friendlier ties between nations; quite another to amalgamate them into a regional, or worse still, world state, and then run the unacceptable risk of centralising power and multiplying man's capacity for mutual destruction.

If the vision of internationalism rather than supra-nationalism is to be our guiding star, what does this imply for Britain and her place in Europe and the world? Only what common sense suggests and existing practice has sanctioned since 1945: namely, membership of appropriate alliances in defence of freedom and the rule of law, and the cultivation of economic interdependence through the liberalisation of European and world trade. Add to that list the need for greater international co-ordination of measures to combat pollution and protect the environment, and you have a sensible model of international co-operation for democracies to follow — though even in the environmental field it is important not to neglect the role that the proper allocation of property rights can play in harnessing personal self-interest to the responsible husbandry of natural resources. The fact that industrial pollution has reached catastrophic levels in the Communist world, where the intrusive power of the State has been unlimited, gives stark emphasis to that point.

At a time when Western Europe needs to open its doors to the emerging post-Communist democracies of the Eastern half of our continent, the vision of a supra-national European state should give way to a more liberal one of an outward-looking Europe of independent nations bound by a common commitment to economic and political liberty, and wedded to forms of international co-operation which do not injure or destroy the diversity which has been the glory of European civilisation. As Wilhelm Röpke, one of Germany's greatest liberal economists, put it in the 1950s:

> In antiquity Strabo spoke of the 'many shapes' of Europe; Montesquieu would speak of Europe as a '*nation des nations*'; Decentrism is of the essence of the spirit of Europe. To try to organise Europe centrally ... and to weld it into a bloc, would be nothing less than a betrayal of Europe and the European patrimony.[11]

# RECOMMENDED READING

*Europe of Many Circles*, by Sir Richard Body MP, New European Publications, London, 1990.
*Enoch Powell on 1992*, edited by Richard Ritchie, Anaya Publishers, London, 1989.
*While Britain Slept: The Selling of the Common Market*, by Douglas Evans, Victor Gollancz, 1975.
*Drift to Union: wiser ways to a wider Community*, by Oliver Letwin, Centre for Policy Studies, 1989.

# NOTES

[1] Speech to Royal Society of St George, 24th April 1933.

[2] Speech to Bruges Group November 1990 Conference.

[3] Speech at Dartford, on the Policy of Lord Salisbury's Second Ministry, 2nd October 1886, from *Speeches of the Rt Hon Lord Randolph Churchill 1880-1888*, collected by Louis J Jennings.

[4] From the poem 'Lord, While For All Mankind We Pray', Dr J. R. Wreford (1800-1881).

[5] *Good Europeans?*, Dr Alan Sked, The Bruges Group, Occasional Paper 4, November 1989.

[6] Two Continents (Disraeli's Speech at Aylesbury, 1859), quoted in *Portrait of England: An Anthology*, Christian Mawson, Penguin Books, 1942.

[7] Quoted in *Enoch Powell on 1992*, edited by Richard Ritchie, Anaya

Publishers, London 1989.

[8] Article in *The Sunday Telegraph*, December 1990.

[9] Ibid.

[10] The Communist holocaust in Russia and China alone has cost between 67 million and 127 million lives this century. For more information about these and other estimates of the human cost of Communism worldwide, see *Idealism Without Illusions: A Foreign Policy for Freedom*, Philip Vander Elst, Freedom Association, London, 1989.

[11]*A Humane Economy*, Wilhelm Röpke, Henry Regnery (1st Eng. edition), 1960.

# The Author

Philip Vander Elst is currently editor of *Freedom Today* and National Branch Organiser of the Freedom Association. He has worked on the staff of the Centre for Policy Studies and the Institute of Economic Affairs and has written widely on political and economic subjects for papers in Britain and the United States — including the *Daily Telegraph,* the *Spectator*, the *Sunday Times*, the *Political Quarterly, Human Events* and the *American Spectator*. Mr Vander Elst read PPE at Oxford and has lectured on these subjects at universities and military academies in the United States. He is a former officer of the Oxford Union Debating Society and has been a writer and broadcaster on radio and television on both sides of the Atlantic. His numerous publications include *Capitalist Technology for Soviet Survival* (Institute of Economic Affairs, 1981) and *The Future of Freedom: Agenda for the 1990s* (Freedom Association, 1987).